"Good Morning Son, time to wake up."
No Sir, once you open your eyes it's time to attack your day.
Awww, thirty more minutes,Dad.
Yes Sir, understood
AF480085

Remember
accountability is key

Yes Sir,
I remember starts
with being responsible.

Speaking of being responsible , why is respect important ?
Because respect is earned not given, also you must respect & love yourself first.

Correct
Can I ask you a question?

Yes Sir, ask away.
When you were young did you have a problem with other's being rude?

Yes sir of course ,
the focus wasn't on them being rude
it was mostly on how I carried myself ,
my parents always taught me
to be mindful of my manners me
Like you always
telling me.

Yes, sir that's correct, that's the power of accountability & responsibility, you must hold yourself to a higher standard, rather becoming the problem let's find solutions.
Yes, sir.

Son,walking in greatness,
that comes with a challenge
in the form of many
test that's the beauty
of it all which unlocks
your superpowers.
Super Powers?

Your brain son haha!
Oh, I see haha!

Remember reading is fun to mental.
You mean fundamental?

Let me explain, the importance of reading allows you to take in information, which in fact tells a story, take you on a journey to explore the writer's thought process also it shares a experience that's subjective, personal, financial etc. basically tools you will be able to apply in life.
Yes sir, I understand just another form of communication.

See son it's my responsibility to prepare you with the knowledge & tools that will kick start your journey into adulthood.
I just want to tell I love you dad, your the worlds greatest.

I love you more son, so son what did you take away from today's conversation ?
Be mindful of what I say , hold myself accountable , be respectful , & reading is a powerful tool of information.

That makes me proud ,
especially knowing you're
on the right path in life ,
trust me you'll do just fine.

I enjoyed it as well son,
love you too ,
you have yourself
a wonderful day.

Well dad I enjoy
this conversation
you and I had love you.

School Bus

www.ingramcontent.com/pod-product-compliance
Lightning Source LLC
Chambersburg PA
CBHW042137110726
48006CB00003B/911